Pachycephalosaurus

Written by Frances Swann
Illustrated by Pam Mara

LIBRARY OF CONGRESS
Library of Congress
Cataloging-in-Publication Data

Swann, Frances, 1955–
    Pachycephalosaurus / by Frances Swann;
illustrated by Pam Mara.
        p.   cm — (Dinosaur library)
    Summary: Describes a day in the life of the
herbivorous Pachycephalosaurus, a dinosaur
who   walked upright and lived in small herds.
Includes   information about its physical
characteristics, habits,   and natural environment.
    ISBN 0-86592-526-7
    1. Pachycephalosaurus—Juvenile literature.
[1. Pachycephalosaurus. 2. Dinosaurs.] I. Mara,
Pamela, ill. II. Title. III. Series.
QE862.O65S932 1988
567.9′7—dc 19   88-5972
                                                 CIP
                                                 AC

Rourke Enterprises, Inc.
Vero Beach, FL 32964

Quetzalcoatlus

Parasaurolphus

Deinosuchus

Corythasaurus

Spinosaurus

Oviraptor

Pachycephalosaurus

Pachycephalosaurus

Anatosaurus

Struthiomimus

Scolosaurus

Rutiodon

Psittacosaurus

It was early morning when Pachycephalosaurus awoke. The air was hot, dry and still.

A little way off, a couple of one year old males were playfighting. Their noise disturbed the others, and slowly the rest of Pachycephalosaurus' small herd began to stir.
The herd had slept in the shelter of a huge overhanging rock on the treeless hillside. It was the dry season. Soon the sun would rise higher, and even in the shadow of the rock it would be uncomfortably hot.

The herd was hungry. They assembled gradually behind Pachycephalosaurus. Slowly they moved down the hillside in search of fresh vegetation and shade.

Pachycephalosaurus felt restless. He was the oldest, largest, and strongest of the males. Therefore, he was the dominant male and the herd leader. This was the mating season, a time when other males would challenge his position. So far he had always won. Pachycephalosaurus knew that one day the outcome would be different, and he would lose his herd to a younger male.

Pachycephalosaurus called his herd in closer. The descent was steep and the ground hard and stony. A Pterosaur flew low over the group. Pachycephalosaurus felt a rush of warm air from its leathery wings. He watched as it glided down toward the valley.

Over the green and yellow treetops he could see the thin blue line of the river. A vast flood plain lay beyond, and the hazy line of a mountain range lay beyond that.

A sudden crack of thunder frightened the herd. They bunched closer together. A lizard darted back into the rocks. The herd quickened its pace.

The descent was less steep now, and the vegetation thicker. The herd stopped to feed on some bushes. Pachycephalosaurus chewed the leaves, but remained watchful. Another clap of thunder shook the valley. Pachycephalosaurus turned. To his horror he saw another Pachycephalosaurus herd standing absolutely still, watching him. In front was a powerful male, his challenging posture unmistakable.

The two males approached each other menacingly, watched by their herds. As the distance between them lessened, both males adopted a butting posture. Heads down, with backs and tails held in a stiff, straight line, they ran at each other.

Their heads met with a dull thud. They retreated and charged at each other again and again. Suddenly the other male withdrew, panting with exhaustion. Pachycephalosaurus had won!

To prove his victory, Pachycephalosaurus chased the challenger and his herd into the thicket of katsura trees. Pachycephalosaurus was shaken, but unhurt.

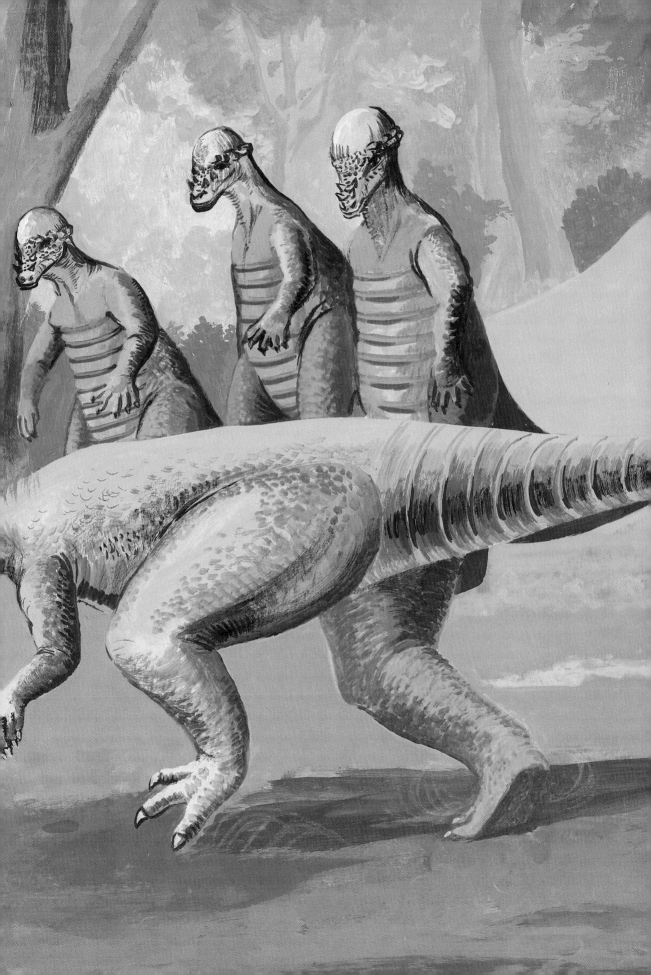

Pachycephalosaurus needed to get his breath back, so the herd moved slowly into the shade of the trees.

The ground was covered with oval yellow katsura leaves. A shrew-like mammal darted out to catch a beetle, and a line of ants swarmed up the trunk of a breadfruit tree. All seemed still.

The herd moved forward. Above them rose the tall silvery bark and the lime green canopy of sycamore trees. A sudden commotion brought the herd to a halt.

Through the trees they could see two male Chasmorsaurus locked in battle. The horns on their great frilled heads clashed together as they pushed and swayed violently.

The Chasmosaurus were intent on their contest, and the herd passed unnoticed.

Pachycephalosaurus grew uneasy as the day continued. A strange smell was in the air. A pair of Stenonychosaurus sprinted back and forth catching insects. They seemed unbothered.

The smell grew stronger, and stronger. Smoke! Pachycephalosaurus was filled with terror. The herd's territory was on the hillside, but the fire had them trapped. Panic stricken, the herd fled deeper into the trees, heading instinctively for the river.

They ran headlong through the thick undergrowth, almost trampling a Panoplosaurus as it lay clutching the ground with alarm.

The smoke was all around them now and the whole forest seemed on the move. The ground shook as a herd of Triceratops charged blindly past them. Small mammals raced across the forest floor, and birds flew wildly above them.

A fleet-footed Struthiomimus raced by, disappearing into the distance. The herd was beginning to tire. Pachycephalosaurus was a large animal and not used to running so far, but terror and panic drove him.

At last the air grew clearer and Pachycephalosaurus could breathe more easily. They were leaving the fire behind.

The herd did not stop until they reached the dry
sandy land by the river. Here they drank and rested, in the
cover of the tall rushes under the redwood trees.

It was late afternoon before Pachycephalosaurus led
his herd out along the river. The air was cooler, sun sparkled on
the water, and all along the bank turtles plopped back into the
river as the herd passed.

Several half submerged crocodiles lay in the shallow
water at the river's edge. Suddenly one stood up. With a fast,
ziz-zagging pace, he made for a clump of tall rushes.

The herd stopped as the dark shape of an angry
female Parasaurolophus rose from her nest. She had been
sitting on her eggs. Her threatening posture, and her size
were too much for the crocodile. It turned back and slid
quietly into the river.

Pachycephalosaurus had no wish to anger the
Parasaurolophus any further. He led his herd around her
nest site, and on through the rushes.

As they rounded the next bend there was a sudden explosion of sound. A deafening mixture of bellows, roars, and splashes filled the air. The herd came to an abrupt halt. Pachycephalosaurus looked wildly about him for the source of the noise.

On the far bank of the river a pack of Dromaeosaurs had killed a Coryothsaurus. Quarrelling among themselves, they were already tearing at their kill.

Thundering toward them was a massive Tyrannosaurus. It roared defiantly, hoping to scatter the Dromaeosaurs and claim the carcass for itself.

Pachycephalosaurus didn't hesitate a moment longer.
The herd turned away from the river and ran back through
the trees.

The acrid smell of smoke still hung over the forest,
but it seemed that they had circled around the center of the
fire.

The light was fading as the herd reached the rocky
hillside. It had been a strange and anxious day for
Pachycephalosaurus.

He watched as his herd settled themselves for the night,
and then, with a soft sigh, he too slept.

The Skeleton of Pachycephalosaurus Compared in Size with a Man

Length 26 ft (8m)

Pachycephalosaurus and the Cretaceous World

The age of the Dinosaurs

The word dinosaur is derived from two Greek words meaning "terrible lizard." All the dinosaurs lived in the Mesozoic era, 225 to 65 million years ago, when the continents were much closer than today. At one time, much of the land was one giant continent called Pangea. This great mass broke up over many millions of years, and segments drifted apart to become our present continents.

No man has ever seen a dinosaur – man did not appear on earth until a mere 2 to 3 million years ago. So how do we know so much about dinosaurs?

Fossil Finds

Our knowledge comes from fossils, which have been discovered all over the world. Fossil skeletons, eggs, nesting sites, tracks, dung, imprints of skin, and even mummified stomach contents have been found. New finds constantly update our view of the dinosaurs and their world.

When Pachycephalosaurus lived

The Mesozoic age is divided into three eras –

Triassic, Jurassic and the Cretaceous. Pachycephalosaurus lived at the end of the Cretaceous era, which lasted from 135 to 65 million years. The word Cretaceous means chalk. During this time great beds of chalk were formed and the continents took on their present shapes. At the start of the Cretaceous era the weather was mild, but by the end it was quite a lot colder.

The land was low-lying, and it was a time of high sea levels, with many delta, rivers, lakes and swamps. Many new types of plants evolved during the Cretaceous era. Flowering plants appeared for the first time. Many of these plants have survived and would be familiar to us today.

All about Pachycephalosaurus

Pachycephalosaurus belonged to a group of dinosaurs called Pachycephalosaurus, meaning "thick headed reptiles." At 26 feet (8m) long, Pachycephalosaurus was the largest of a group of thirteen known types. These have been found as widely apart as North America, Asia, England and Madagascar.

Pachycephalosaurus was a herbivore (plant eater) who walked upright on its hind legs. It probably lived in small herds in the drier highland areas, much as goats do today.

Pachycephalosaurus had a high domed skull with a massively thickened skull roof. It is presumed that the males would have defended their territories by having "head-butting" contests. Present day goats and rams behave the same way.

Pachycephalosaurus lived 75 to 64 million years ago. The relationship of Pachycephalosaurus to other groups of dinosaurs is still unclear.

Other Dinosaurs in this Book

All the dinosaurs in this book lived in North America in the late Cretaceous era.

CHASMOSAURUS

17 feet, (5.2m) long dinosaur from Alberta, Canada and New Mexico. Chasmosaurus was a ceratopid dinosaur. A huge horned frill covered its neck and back. Chasmosaurus also had three large facial horns. The frill was probably used to display behavior. The horns were defensive weapons, and may have been used, much like antlers, in the pushing contests between males.

STENONYCHOSAURUS

A 6.5 feet, (2m) long dinosaur from Alberta. This fast, lightly built dinosaur had a large, well developed brain. It lived on small animals, possibly mammals and lizards. Its large eyes may have helped it hunt its prey in dim light.

PANOPLOSAURUS

Panoplosaurus was a North American dinosaur. Panoplosaurus was a very heavily armored dinosaur. Only incomplete fossil skeletons have been found, but we do have well preserved skulls. Panoplosaurus was a plant eater. Under attack, Panoplosaurus would have withdrawn its legs and clutched the ground, presenting a predator with only its armored "shell".

CORYTHOSAURUS

A 33 feet (10m) long dinosaur, similar in shape and size to a Parasaurolophus. Corythosaurus had a helmet shaped crest.

TYRANNOSAURUS

A 39 feet (12m) long dinosaur from North America. Tyrannosaurus was massive, the biggest flesh eating dinosaur: Tyrannosaurus was about 18 feet (5.6m) high, and weighed about 7 tons. Tyrannosaurus may have lived mainly off dead animals since its huge size probably made hunting difficult. Some scientists believe Tyrannosaurus was agile and fast enough to catch its own prey.

PTERANODON

Pteranodon was not a dinosaur, but a flying reptile, a pterosaur. One type of pterosaur called Quzalcoatlus had a 50 foot (15m) wing span. This is the same size as a small light aircraft!

DROMAEOSAURUS

A 6 feet (1.8m) long dinosaur from Alberta. Only the head, arms, and legs of this dinosaur have been found. It was a carnivore that probably hunted with others in a pack. Each hind leg had one huge claw which would have been used to disable its prey.

STRUTHIOMIMUS

Struthiomimus was a 10 to 13 foot (3–4m) long dinosaur. Know as an "ostrich dinosaur," it was capable of great speed and agility. It was an omnivore, that is, an animal that eats both plants and meat. Under attack Struthiomimus would have been able to outrun a predator. Fossil remains of Struthiomimus have been found in Alberta.

PARASAUROLOPHUS

Parasaurolophus was a dinosaur from North America. It had a very long tubular crest. This crest was probably used as a visual signal to others in the group, and as a resonator for producing a trumpeting call. Parasaurolophus had a wide, deep tail, and paddle-like hands. Under attack it could escape a predator by swimming. This type of dinosaur was known as a hadrosaurid.

TRICERATOPS

A 30 feet (9m) long dinosaur that could weigh up to 5.4 tons. Triceratops remains have been found all over North America. Triceratops was a short-frilled ceratopian dinosaur. It had three sharp facial horns. Under attack it may have charged its attacker in the same way as our present day rhino.